1970-1980 One Hundred Greatest Hits

Piano-Vocal-Guitar

Wise Publications
London/New York/Sydney/Tokyo/Cologne

Exclusive distributors:
Music Sales Limited
8/9 Frith Street, London W1V 5TZ, England.
Music Sales Pty. Limited
120 Rothschild Avenue, Rosebery, NSW 2018, Australia

This book © Copyright 1980 by
Wise Publications
ISBN 0.86001.701.X
Order No:.AM 22591

Music Sales complete catalogue lists thousands
of titles and is free from your local music
book shop, or direct from Music Sales Limited.
Please send £ 1 in stamps for postage to
Music Sales Limited, 8/9 Frith Street, London, W1V 5TZ.

Typeset by DahDah Typesetters Limited. London.
Printed in Austria

Just The Way You Are

Words and Music by Billy Joel

And I don't see___ you___ an - y more___

___ I___ would___ not leave you___ in times of

trou-ble___ We nev - er could have come___ this far___

___ mm ___ mm ___ I took the good___ times___

I'll take the bad ___ times ___   I'll take you just ___

___ the way ___ you are ___

Don't go try-ing

Some ___ new fash - ion ___   Don't change the col -

or of your hair___ mm___ mm___ You al - ways

have my un - spok - en pas - sion___

Al - though I might___ not seem to care___

I___ don't___ want clev - er___ con - ver-

sa-tion ___   I nev-er   want to work ___ that hard ___

mm ___ mm ___ I just want some-one ___ that I can talk ___

___ to ___   I want you just ___ the way ___ you are. ___

I need to know___ that you___ will al - ways be___

The same old some - one that I knew___ Oh

What will___ it take___ till you___ be - lieve___ in me___

___ The way that I___ be - lieve___ in you___

the way__ you are _____

D. S. al Coda

Coda

I _____ don't__ want clev-er__

con - ver - sa - tion I nev - er

Ain't No Stopping Us Now

Words and Music by
John Whitehead, Gene McFadden and Jerry Cohen

but now it looks like things are fin-al-ly com-in' a-round
and if you're try-in' to make it they on-ly push you a-side

Bbm7   Cm7   Fm7

I know we've got a long long way to go.
They real-ly don't have no-where to go.

Bbm7   Cm7   Fm7

and where we'll end up, I don't know but we won't let no-thin'
ask them where they're go-in' they don't know.

Bbm7   Cm7   Fm7   Bbm

hold us back we're put-tin' our show to-ge-ther we're pol-ish-ing up our act well

Cm7   Fm7   Bbm7   Cm7   Fm7

and if you ev-er___ been held down be-fore I know you'd re-fuse to be

Bbm7　　　　　　　　　Cm7　　Fm7　　　　Bbm7

held down a - ny-more　　　　　Don't you let　no - thin' no - thin'

Cm7　　Fm7　　　　　Absus4

stand in your way,___　　　　　　　　　I want y'all to

D.C.

lis - ten lis - ten　　　　to ev-er-y word I say　ev - er-y word I say.

Fmsus4

Ring My Bell

Words and Music by Frederick Knight

Ain't Love A Bitch

Words and Music by
Rod Stewart and Gary Grainger

You're driv-ing home late one night,_ and on the ra - di - o_

comes an old, fa - mil-iar song_ you used to know so well._

Oh, I_ can't com - pre-hend_ this thing called love.

May-be_ it's a mat-ter of fact_ I just can't grow up._

23

Deep down, ain't we all a lit-tle ju-ven-ile.

All I real-ly want to know: Is there

one sweet an-gel that can make me smile? Tor-

freely

a tempo

ren-tial rains, wars and hur-ri-canes. I would-n't budge an inch.

24

Your rent's un-paid and your team lose a-gain.— But ain't love a bitch.— You can lose your job, your home and your head..But ain't love a bitch.— Take it or leave it. Some-day you'll feel it.'Cause *love is the bitch.*

Repeat and fade

Sweet Gingerbread Man

Words by Alan and Marilyn Bergman
Music by Michel Legrand

28

Alone Again (Naturally)

Words and Music by
Raymond O'Sullivan

Year Of The Cat

Words and Music by
Al Stewart and Peter Wood

in the year of the cat.___
the year of the cat."___
in the year of the cat.__

She

Well, she looks at you___ so cool - ly and her eyes shine like the

moon in the sea.___ She comes in in - cense and patch - ou - li. So you

Don't It Make My Brown Eyes Blue

Words and Music by Richard Leigh

Y.M.C.A.

Words and Music by
J. Morali, H. Belolo and V. Willis

Chorus: It's fun to stay at the Y.. M. C. A.

(1st D.S.S. Instrumental) – – – – – – – –

It's fun to stay at the ____ Y. M. C. A. ____

_____ They have ev - er - y - thing ____ for young

men to en - joy. ____ You can hang out with all ____ the boys. ____

have a good meal.
need to feel down.
list-'ning to me?

You can do what-ev-er you feel

Young man, young man

{ pick your-
{ what do

self off the ground. you want to be?

Verse 3 :   Young man, are you listening to me?
            I said, young man what do you want to be?
            I said, young man you can make real your dreams
            But you've got to know this one thing.

Verse 4 :   No man does it all by himself.
            I said young man put your pride on the shelf.
            And just go there to the Y.M.C.A.
            I'm sure they can help you today.
            (To Chorus:)

Verse 5 :   Young man I was once in your shoes
            I said, I was down and out and with the blues.
            I felt no man cared if I were alive.
            I felt the whole world was so jive.

Verse 6 :   That's when someone come up to me
            And said, "Young man, take a walk up the street.
            It's a place there called the Y.M.C.A.
            They can start you back on your way."
            (To Chorus:)

We Don't Talk Anymore

Words and Music by Alan Tarney

Arms Of Mary

Words and Music by
Iain Sutherland

The lights shine down the val - ley
So now when I get lone - ly

The wind blows
still look - ing for the

up the al - ley, Oh _____ well I wish I was ly - ing in the arms of Mar -
one and on - ly, _____ That's when I wish I was ly - ing in the arms of Mar -

- y.
- y.

She took the pains of boy - hood,
(2nd time – Instrumental) _____

and turned them in - to feel good Oh how I wish I was

C   F   C

ly - ing in the arms of Mar - y. *(Vocal both times)* Mar - y was the girl who taught me all I

G   C   Em

had to know she put me right on my first mis - take Summer was-n't

Am   F   G

gone when I learned all she had to show she real - ly gave all a boy could take

Em   Am   F

Oh — The lights shine down the val-ley

The wind blows up the al-ley Oh — well I wish I was ly-ing in the arms of Mar

-y. Ly-ing in the arms of Mar-y, ly-ing in the arms of Mar-y.

5 times (Vocal 1st time)

Ooh ooh — ooh

Moonraker

Words by Hal David
Music by John Barry

touch and it al - ways seems____ you

love me. You love

me._____

me.

50

Night Owl

Words and Music by Gerry Rafferty

Night comes down ___ and finds you a - lone ___ in a space ___ in time of your own ___
___ and the mu-zak is loud ___ you watch your - self ___ as you play to the crowd ___
(Inst.3rd & 4th times)

___ lost in dreams ___ in a world full of shad - ows. ___
one more face ___ in a pal - ace of mir - rors. ___

Down the street ___ the ne - on light shines ___ off-'ring ref - uge and hope ___ to the blind, ___
one more drink ___ you're steal-ing a - way ___ one more dream, ___ but it's look-ing o - kay, ___

___ you stum - ble in ___ with no thought of to - mor - row. ___
one more time ___ to watch the flow of the riv - er. ___

CHORUS

Yes, I ___ get lone - ly when the sun gets low, ___ and I ___
(vocal 3x)

___ end up look-ing for some - where to go. ___ Yes, I ___ should know bet-ter, but I

She Believes In Me

Words and Music by Steve Gibb

Streets Of London

Words and Music by Ralph McTell

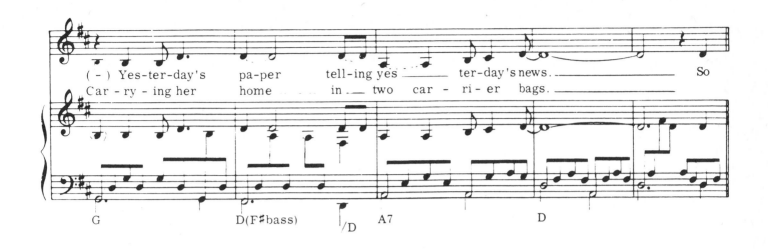

(-) Yes-ter-day's pa-per tell-ing yes ___ ter-day's news. ___ So
Car - ry - ing her home in __ two car - ri - er bags. ___

G   D(F#bass)   /D   A7   D

CHORUS

hcw can you tell __ me you're lone ___ ly   And say for you.

G   D   D/F#   A7   Bm   Bm7/A   E7/G#

___ that the sun don't shine? ___   Let me take_ you   by the hand __ and

A7   D   A(C#bass)

lead you through __ the streets of Lon-don.   I'll show you some-thing ___ to make you change _your

Bm   F#m(Abass)   G   D(F#bass)   A7

61

2. In the all —— night ca - fé   at a quart-er past —— e - lev - en
3. Have you seen —— the   old man   out - side the sea - man's miss-ion,

And say for you___ that the sun don't shine?___

E7/G#   A7

Let me take___ you by the hand___ and lead you through ___ the streets of Lon - don.

D   A(C#bass)   Bm   F#m(Abass)

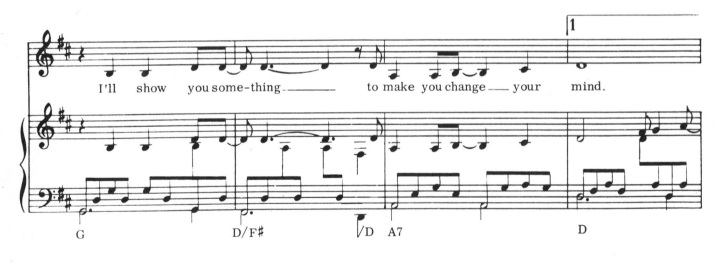

I'll show you some-thing___ to make you change___ your mind.

G   D/F#   /D A7   D

1

mind.

Rall......

A/C#   Bm   A7(sus)   A7   D

2

In The Navy

Words and Music by
J. Morali, H. Belolo and V. Willis

Where can you learn to fly, play-ing sports or skin - dive
May - be you are too young to join up to-day but

stu - dy oc - ean - og - raph-y. ___ Sign up for the big band or ___
don't you wor - ry 'bout a thing ___ for I'm sure there will be al -

___ sit in the grand-stand when your team and oth - ers meet. ___
- ways the good na - vy pro - tect-ing the land and sea. ___ (In the

CHORUS

na - vy ___) yes, you can sail the sev-en seas ___ (in the na - vy ___) yes, you can

put your mind at ease _ (in the na - vy _____) come on now, peo-ple make a stand _ (in the

na - vy _____) can't you see we need a hand. _ (in the na - vy _____) come, on, pro-

tect the moth-er-land _ (in the na - vy _____) come on and join your fel - low man _ (in the

na - vy _____) come on peo - ple and make a stand _ (in the na - vy ____), in the

na - vy,   in the na - vy.

(They want you,   they want you,   they want you as   a   new   re - cruit.)

they want you as   a   new   re - cruit.)   They want you,   they want you,
(who   me?)

they want you as   a   new   re - cruit.   (Spoken ad lib.)   But ___

He's The Greatest Dancer

Words and Music by
Nile Rodgers and Bernard Edwards

71

Honesty

Words and Music by Billy Joel

Hot Stuff

Words and Music by
Pete Bellotte, Harold Faltermeyer and Keith Forsey

Sit-ting here eat-ing my heart____ out wait-ing,
Look-ing for a lov-er who needs____ an-oth-er, don't

wait-ing for some lov-er to call.____
want an-oth-er night on my own.____

Dialled a-bout a thou-sand num-
Wan-na share my love with a warm-

bers late-ly,
-er lov-er,

al-most dragged the 'phone off the wall.
wan-na bring a wild man back

CHORUS

home.
Got-ta have some (2) hot love ba-by, this eve-
Look-ing for some (1) hot stuff ba-by, this eve-
(3) hot stuff ba-by, this eve-

I need hot stuff
I need hot stuff,   I want some
I   I want some

hot stuff   I need hot stuff._____
hot love,   look-ing for hot love._____

83

So You Win Again

Words and Music by Russ Ballard

So you win a - gain___ you win a - gain___ Here I stand a - gain___

E A/E E   E+/G♯ A   F♯m   Bm

the los - er   And just for fun___ you took my love and run___ but love had just be-gun___

Dm   A   F♯m   Bm

I can't re-fuse her but now I know___ that I'm the fool___ who won your love,___ to

F♯   Bm   D   A

lose it all___ when you come back   you'll win a - gain___ (Doo doo doo

F♯   Bm7   E   A

To Coda ⊕

doo doo doo doo   doo doo doo doo)   And I'm not proud to say___

F♯m   Bm   E   E/G♯ A

85

Rasputin

Words and Music by
Farian, Reyam and Jay

He could preach the bi-ble like a preach-er full of ex-ta-sy and fire.
For the Queen he was no wheeler-deal-er though she heard the things he'd done
Then one night some men of high-er stand-ing set a trap, they're not to blame

But he al-so was the kind of teach-er wo-men would de-sire.
She be-lieved he was a ho-ly heal-er who would heal her son.
"Come to vi-sit us" they kept de-man-ding and he real-ly came.

GIRLS 1, 2. Ra-ra ras-pu-tin lo-ver of the Russian queen there was a cat that real-ly was gone
MAN 3. Ra-ra ras-pu-tin lo-ver of the Russian queen they put some pois-on in-to his wine

To Coda ⊕

GIRLS 1, 2. Ra-ra ras-pu-tin Rus-sia's great-est love machine it was a shame how he car-ried on.
MAN 3. Ra-ra ras-pu-tin Rus-sia's great-est love-machine he drank it all and said "I feel fine."

Spoken: But when his drinkin' and lusting, and his hunger for power became known to more and more people, the demands to do

something about this outrageous man became louder and louder!

Hey hey hey hey hey hey hey hey hey hey hey hey hey hey hey hey hey hey hey hey

1. Ra - ra - ras - pu - tin lo - ver of the Rus - sian queen they did - n't quit, they
2. Ra - ra - ras - pu - tin Rus - sia's great - est love ma - chine and so they shot him

want - ed his head. __ till he was dead. _____ *Spoken:* Oh those Russians!

Bad, Bad, Leroy Brown

Words and Music by Jim Croce

Thank You For The Music

Words and Music by
Benny Andersson and Bjorn Ulvaeus

all I want ___ is to sing ___ it out loud. ___ So I say
Well, who e- ___ ver it was, ___ I'm a fan. ___

Thank you for the mu-sic, the songs I'm sing-ing. Thanks for all the joy they're bringing.

Who can live with-out it? I ask in all ho-nes-ty. ___ What would life be ___

___ with-out a song ___ or dance, ___ what are we? So I say

thank you for the mu-sic, for giv-ing it to me. ___

Fairytale

Words and Music by Paul Greedus

97

you and on - ly you a - lone__ be - lieve they__ do.__

C

F

D.S. repeat chorus ad lib., and fade

2. You're

Lucky Stars

Words and Music by Dean Friedman

Verse 3

Baby, I'm sorry I was wrong – I have no alibis.
I was acting like a fool and I apologise.
Listen hon', I know you're dumb but that's O.K.
You don't have to look so glum – Do you still love me?
      Yes, I still love you.
– You mean you're not being nice? – I'm not just being nice.
Do you feel sleepy? – Oh you're so sincere!
Yes, I feel sleepy – Then slide over here 'cause
I may not be all that bright but I know how to hold you tight
And you can thank your lucky stars
That we're not as smart as we'd like to think we are
And you can thank your lucky stars that we're
Not as smart as we'd like to think we are
And we can thank our lucky stars that we're
Not as smart as we'd like to think we are.

The Name Of The Game

Words and Music by
Benny Andersson, Stig Anderson and Bjorn Ulvaeus

Tell me please ___ 'cause I have to know, ___ I'm a bash-ful child ___ be-

ginning to grow. ___ And you make me talk, ___ And you make me feel, ___

___ And you make me show ___ what I'm try-ing to ___ conceal. If I trust in you ___ would you

let me down, ___ would you laugh at me? ___ If I said I care ___ for you

could you feel the same ___ way too? I wanna know ___ the name of the game

We're All Alone

Words and Music by Boz Scaggs

dream will take us out to sea ____ for -
hours long for - got - ten now, ____ we're
cast your sea - sons to the wind, ____ and

ev - er - more, _____ for - ev - er - more. __
all a - lone, _____ we're all a - lone. __
hold me, dear, _____ oh, hold me, dear. __

Close the win - dow, calm the light, ____ and it will be ____ all

Summer Breeze

Words and Music by
James Seals and Darrell Crofts

blow-in through the jas-mine in my mind_____ all in your mind._____

Dm7   G11   C   Bm7   E

See the cur-tains hang-ing in the win-dow   in the ev'-ning   on a Fri-day night;_
See the smile   wait-ing in the kit-chen   good cook-ing,   and a pa-per too;_

A   C   G   D

A lit-tle light shin-ing through the win-dow,   lets me know ev'-ry,   ev'-ry-thing's al-
feel the arms reach-in' out   to hold me,   in the ev-en-ing,   when the day is

A   C   A   C   G   D

ri-i-i-i-i-i-ght.
thr-ou-ou-ou-ou-ou-gh.   Sum-mer breeze   makes me feel fine_____

A   Dm7   Em7

Sorry I'm A Lady

Words by Frank Dostal
Music by Rolf Soja

Chanson D'Amour

Words and Music by Wayne Shanklin

da,   More   and more.

Chan   son   d'a - mour   Ra da da da

da,   Je   t'a - dore.

Each   time   I hear

Ra da da da da chan - son, ___ chan -son ___

d'a - mour. ___

Cm   C#dim   F7

Bb   Cm7 Bdim Cm7   F7

Ev - 'ry-time I hear chan-son, ___ chan - son ___

d'a - mour. ___

Bb   F7

Bb

Angelo

Words and Music by
Tony Hiller, Lee Sheriden and Martin Lee

Medium tempo

Long a - go, high on a mount-ain in Mex-i-co, lived a young shep-herd boy,

An-gel-o, who met a young girl and he loved her so.

1. Rich was she came from a ve-ry high fam-i-ly, An-gel-o knew it could
2. Long a - go, high on a mount-ain in Mex-i-co, lived a young shep-herd boy

ne - ver be, they ran a - way to their dest - in-y_____
An-gel - o who met a young girl and he loved her so_____

A♭   G7

Run-ning a - way__ to-geth-er, run-ning a - way__ for - ev - er, An - gel - o_____

C   Fmaj7   F

_____ Run-ning a - way__ from dan - ger, hid - ing from ev - 'ry strang-er,

Fmaj7   F   C

An - gel - o_____ They knew it was - n't wrong,__ they found a

Fmaj7   F   Fmaj9   F   C

love so strong they took their lives __ that night __ And in the morn - ing light __ they found them

on __ the sand, __ they saw them ly - ing there __ hand in hand __

Take A Chance On Me

Words and Music by
Benny Andersson and Bjorn Ulvaeus

If you put me to ___ the test if you let me try, ___ take a

chance on me, ___ take a chance on me, ___

2. Oh you can take your time ba- by. We can go ___ danc - ing, we can go walk - ing ___ as

long as we're ___ to - get - her
know I'm gon - na get ___ you
lis - ten to ___ some mu - sic
you don't wan - na hurt ___ me

may - be just ___ talk - ing ___ you'd get to know ___ me bet - ter
ba - by don't ___ wor - ry ___ I ain't gon - na let ___ you

If you need me let me know gonna be a-round. If you got no place to go when you're feel-ing down. If you're all a-lone when the pret-ty birds have flown Ho-ney I'm still free, take a chance on me gonna do my ve-ry best ba-by can't you see gotta put me to the test take a chance on me. If you change your mind

Repeat
and Fade

Wild West Hero

Words and Music by Jeff Lynne

126

A-Ba-Ni-Bi

Words and Music by
Ehud Manor and Nurit Hirsh

my days were hap-py, free and wild.   But when in love I could-n't say

Gm   Cm   B♭

the words I wanna say to-day.   Those words were al-ways spin-ning in my head,
                                            I wan - na say the words of yes-ter-day,

Gm   Cm   B♭

I used to whisper them at night in bed. _   And when a-lone I didn't try   to hide _
I wan-na love you in the same old way. _   The words of love are coming close to shore_

Gm   Cm   B♭

those mag-ic words I kept in - side.
so   let me say   them more and more.   A-ba-ni-bi o-bo-he - bev

Gm   Cm tacet. . . . .*Fm

129

Walkin' In The Rain With The One I Love

Words and Music by Barry White

One — I Love — on — my mind.

To each — his own — I've heard — them say, —

Well, I've — got mine — in so man - y ways. —

1. Like be-ing to-geth - er, *(Spoken)*
2. So in love with each oth - er,

Whether near or far, it doesn't matter where you are.
With every passing day we share the thought of knowing
someone cares.

Miss You Nights

Words and Music by Dave Townsend

It's on-ly me__ whose killing time.

(Play down __) play down all dreams and

Gm   C   Bb   C

themes once re-mem-bered

It's just the same __

This miss you game

Am   Dm   Bb   Csus4   C7

Yet these

F   Dm   Bb   F   C

miss you nights

are the long-est __

Bb   Gm7/C   C   Gm/F F

Love's Unkind

Words and Music by
Donna Summer, Giorgio Moroder and Pete Bellotte

Well, I

Bb   F7

see him ev - 'ry morn - ing in the   school-yard 'fore the school ___ bell
just the oth - er day ___ I was pray - ing he would give me a chance, ___

141

Way Down

Words and Music by Layng Martine Jnr.

way down like a ti-dal wave.___ Way down where the fir-es blaze,___ way

down._____ down,_____ way, way on

down, (way on down) down)

Hold me a-gain as tight___

145

If You Know What I Mean

Words and Music by Neil Diamond

From a - no-ther time__ from a - no-ther place,__ Do you re-
It was a - no-ther time__ it was a - no-ther place,__ Do you re-

mem-ber it babe?
mem-ber it babe?

Chorus

And the ra - di - o played like a car-ni-val tune as we lay in our bed in the o - ther

room, when we gave it a-way for the sake of a dream in a pen-ny ar-cade, If you know what I

To Coda

D.S. al Coda

arms a - gain and hard to let them go._____ Do you

⊕ CODA

mean. If you know what I

cresc. poco a poco

mean; If you know what I mean;

If you know what I mean.

150

Don't Bring Me Down

Words and Music by Jeff Lynne

Moderately, with an old-fashioned rock 'n' roll beat

1. You got me run-nin', go-in' out of my mind,___
2. You wan-na stay out with your fan-cy friends,___
3. What hap-pened to the girl I used to know?___
4. You're al-ways talk-in' 'bout your cra-zy nights,___
5. You're look-in' good just like a snake in the grass,___
6. You got me shak-in', got me run-nin' a-way,___

You got me think-in' that I'm wast-in' my time. ___
I'm tell-in' you it's got to be the end. ___
You let your mind out some-where down the road. ___
One of these days you're gon-na get it right. ___
One of these days you're gon-na break your glass. ___
You got me crawl-in' up to you ev-'ry day. ___

Don't Bring Me

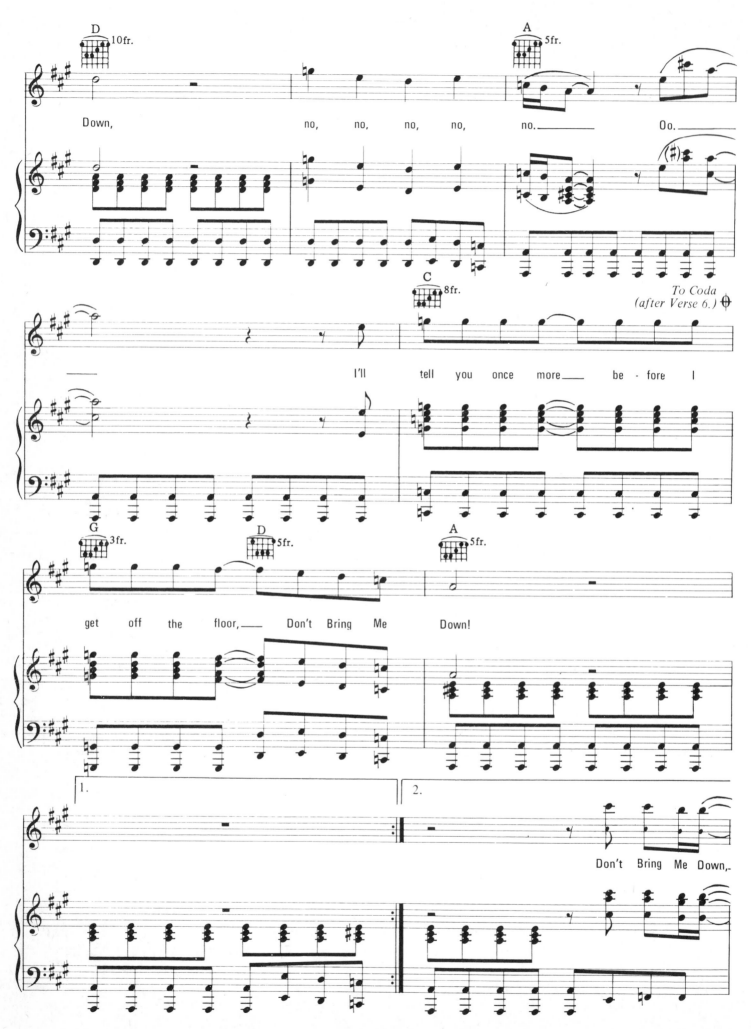

Down,   no,   no,   no,   no,   no.   Oo.

To Coda
(after Verse 6.)

I'll   tell   you   once   more   be - fore   I

get   off   the   floor,   Don't   Bring   Me   Down!

1.

2.

Don't   Bring   Me   Down,-

152

grroosss,— Don't Bring Me Down,_____ grroosss,—

Don't Bring Me Down,_____ grroosss,— Don't Bring Me Down,_

1st time: D.S. al Verses 3. & 4.
2nd time: D.S. al Verses 5. & 6. al Coda

Coda

No Chord

get off the floor,_ Don't Bring Me Down!

8va bassa ------------- ⌐

153

Don't Go Breaking My Heart

Words and Music by
Ann Orson and Carte Blanche

Contact

Words and Music by
Edwin Starr, Arthur E. Pullam and Robert Dickerson

catch the dis - co fev - er
fought my way ov - er.
and then she raised her head, her eyes
I nev - er took my eyes a - way

____ caught mine ___ and that was all ___ that I need - ed. In her eyes
from yours, not ev - en _____ for a mom - ent. What I saw___

____ in your ___ eyes _____
____ made me ___ re - a - lize _____
I saw the need for love,___
warm, soft, plead-
you, I want-

CHORUS

ing.
ed.
Eye to eye___ con - tact

me.

(2) A-

Con-tact!

(3) Girl don't you get up - tight, let's dance. __

ev-e-ry day's

____ gon - na be al - right, __ let's dance. __

163

Does Your Mother Know

Words and Music by
Benny Andersson and Bjorn Ulvaeus

Medium rock

VERSE

1. You're so hot teas-ing me so you're blue, but I can't take a
2. I can see what you want but you seem pret-ty young to be

chance on a chick like you, it's some-thing I could-n't do.
search - ing for that kind of fun, so may - be I'm not the one.

1.

nice and slow (does your mo - ther   know?).

2.

mo - ther   know?).

G   Cm/G   G   Cm/G   G   Cm/G

Well, I could dance with you, ho - ney, if   you think it's fun - ny, does

8va optional
G   C

your mo-ther know that you're out?   And I could chat   with you, ba - by, flirt

G   C   Csus

Repeat and fade out

a lit - tle may-be, does   your mo-ther know that you're out?   Well, I could

C   Csus   C   G

Hanging On The Telephone

Words and Music by Jack Lee

170

Bright Eyes

Words and Music by Mike Batt

sud-den-ly burn_ so pale?_ Bright_ eyes._

bright _ eyes, _ Bright _ eyes._

D.%. (no repeat) al Coda

poco rit.

Can't Smile Without You

Words and Music by
Chris Arnold, David Martin and Geoff Morrow

Now it all seems light-years a-way. And now you know I can't smile with-out you. I can't smile with-out you. I can't laugh and I can't sing. I'm find-ing it hard__ to do an-y-thing.__ You see, I feel sad when you're sad.

178

Clair

Words and Music by Raymond O'Sullivan

look up and smile___ I don't care what peo-ple say___ to me, you're

hear-ing you say___ I'm going to mar - ry you, will___ you mar - ry

Bb9   Ab6

Dal 𝄋 al Coda

more than a child___ oh   Clair   Clair _____

me Un-cle Ray___ oh   Clair   Clair _____

Bb9   Bbm7   Eb9   Eb9

CODA   Solo

F#m7   Bm7   E7

Amaj7   D#m7(b5)   C#maj7

cap-ture my breath,—what there is left of it.—— You can be mur——der at this

hour of the day,—— but in the morn—ing, to-night—— will seem a

life-time a-way,—— Oh Clair   Clair ———   Clair ———

Oh Clair.

poco a poco

You Don't Bring Me Flowers

Words by Neil Diamond, Marilyn Bergman and Alan Bergman
Music by Neil Diamond

Music Box Dancer

Piano Solo by Frank Mills

Sometimes When We Touch

Words and Music by
Dan Hill and Barry Mann

times I'd like ___ to break ___ you   and drive you to ___ your knees, _____   at

G11   Cmaj7

times I'd like _____ to break _____ through ___   and hold _____ you end - less - ly.

Am   Em   F

D. S. al Coda   ⊕ *CODA*

And   ___ in me ___ sub-sides..

G11   G11

rall.

C   G/C   F   C

197

Talking In Your Sleep

Words and Music by
Roger Cook and Bobby Wood

1. Three o' clock in the morn-ing and it looks like it's gon-na be a-noth-er
2. 3. Ba - by I'm be-ing fool - ish 'cos I have-n't heard you mention an-y -bo - dy's

sleep - less night ___ I've been listen-ing to your dreams and ___ get-tin' ve - ry low ___
name at all ___ How I wish I could be sure it's ___ me that turns_you on ___

wonder-in' what I ___ can do ___ Each time you

close your eyes   I've heard it said that dream-ers nev-er lie

Bb7/D   Bb7   Bbm   Cm7   Bbm/Db   Bbm7/F   Ab

CHORUS

You've been talk-in' in___ your___ sleep   sleep-in'   in your___

Bbm7

___ dreams _____ with some___ sweet lo-ver

Cm7   Db   Ab/Eb   Eb7

Hold-ing on___ so___ tight___ lov-in'   her the way___

Ab   Bbm7

you used to ___ love me

talk - in' in ___ your ___ sleep with lov - in' on ___

your ___ mind ___

your ___ mind ___ You've been talk - in' in ___ your ___ sleep

You Light Up My Life

Words and Music by Joe Brooks

lone in the dark, but now you've come a - long. And
nev - er a - gain to be all a - lone

you light up my life. You give me hope, to car - ry on. You light up my days and fill my

nights _____ with song. _____

nights _____ with song. _____

nights with song. It can't be wrong_____ when

it feels so right, _____ 'cause you

_____ you light up my _____ life. _____

My Sweet Rosalie

Words and Music by
Tony Hiller, Lee Sheriden and Martin Lee

and ve - ry much to my_ sur - prise____ some - one
-er ___ 'cos we're such a per -fect pair__ and when I

D   Bm   F#m

kissed me,   made me op - en up__ my eyes ____   I
want her   — I know she's al - ways there.__   She's

Em7   A11   A7

turned a - round_ to solve__ this my - ster - y _____
ev' - ry - thing_ a guy__ could ev - er need, _____

G   G6   Gmaj7

And who d'ya think_ was sit - tin' next to me?
I love her, oh I love her yes in - deed.

G   E7(sus4)   E7

Uptown Uptempo Woman

Words and Music by Randy Edelman

It start-ed out in in - no-cence the way that most things do

A thousand peo-ple crammed in one place but the on-ly face was you

I took your hand and we raced out_ hard-ly said a word_

Bb   Bb/D   Cm7

I'd on-ly seen you for_ a minute but I was round in third And we

Fsus4   F7   Eb   F7   Bb

trad-ed on_ our back-grounds you men-tioned I seemed shy Then you

Dm   Eb   Fsus4

laughed and said_"I'm an up-town up-tem-po wo-man you're a
up-town up-tem-po wo-man find the

Bb   Bb/D

down-town down-beat guy.
down-town down-beat guy.

Cm7   F7   Bb/D   Gm

Cm7   F7   Bb   Bb/D

To coda ⊕ *(for verse 4)*

With - in a week I'd moved in
Well the ro-mance soon was ov - er

Cm7   F7   Bb   Bb/D

at her up-town east-side place
and the lust was turn-ing thin

We'd make love for hours _____ on a
And I soon be-gan to re - a - lize the

Cm7   Fsus4   F7

bed of silk and lace___
mess that I was in___
She would get up ear-ly
But as al-ways hap-pens
and
when you're

Eb   Fsus4   F7   Bb   Bb/D

come home late at night.
caught in such a trap___
She had im-portant bus'-ness
You get so used to what's around
But my
That you

Cm7   Fsus4   F7

pros - pects all seemed slight
can't find your way back
So I

Eb   F7   Bb

And ti-red on some eve-ning
lived with this ar - rangement
she'd get mad and cry
soon learned to des - pise
I'm an
The

Dm   Eb   Fsus4   F7

But this day she was ear - ly

she looked at me and asked "why?"

Eb

I said "why"?

You're an

Fsus4

F7

up-town up-tem-po wo-man   and I'm a   down-town down-beat   guy

Bb

Bb/D

Cm7

F7

Bb/D

Gm

Repeat and fade

You're an   up-town up-tem-po wo-man   and I'm a

Cm7

F7

Bb

Bb/D

You're In My Heart
Words and Music by Rod Stewart

4. The big bos-omed la-dy with the Dutch ac-cent who tried to change my point of view
6. You're a rhap-so-dy, a com-e-dy, you're a sym-phon-y and a play

her ad lib lines were well re-hearsed, but my heart cried out for you.
you're ev'-ry love song ev-er writ-ten, but hon-ey, what do you see in me?

CHORUS

You're in my heart, you're in my soul, you'll be my breath should I grow

To Coda

old, you are my lov - er, you're my best friend, you're in my soul.

7. You're an essay in glamour,—please pardon the grammar,
    But you're ev'ry schoolboy's dream,
    You're Celtic, United, but baby I've decided
    You're the best team I've ever seen.

8. And there have been many affairs
    Many times I thought to leave,
    But I bite my lip and turn around 'cos
    You're the warmest thing I've ever found.

    (to chorus - repeat)

Song For Guy

By Elton John

219

Life is - n't ev - er - y - thing, _____

is - n't ev - er - y - thing,   is - n't ev - er - y -

Three times

Three times

What Can I Say

Words and Music by
Boz Scaggs and David Paich

lonely, dear___   I've been feel - in' down some too___

Am6   Am9   Am6

Af - ter all_ this time now   ain't it clear___   I've been wait-ing just for you. __

Am9   Am6/9   Am9   Am

CHORUS

1. What can I say ___   oh to make you know ___ ba - by What can I do ___
2. What can I say ___ ooh you got me act - ing like a fool, girl What can I do ___ Stop

G   Bm7   Am7   G   Bm7

To Coda ✛

show you that I care _____ What can I say ___   got to have your num - ber, ba - by
mak-in' like a lit - tle school -girl   What can I say ___ could be your luck - y day, ba - by

Am7   G   Bm7   Am7

What can I do. —

Can't you see — the peo-ple   just   stop and stare — Don't it make you wonder   why —

I just happened to be   stand-ing there   Can't you see it in   my   eyes. —

D.S. (twice),
take Coda last time

Repeat ad lib. and fade

⊕ CODA

What can I say —   oh to make you know   ba-by What can I do —   show   you that I care —
What can I say ooh you got me act-ing like a fool girl   What can I do stop mak-in' like a lit-tle school girl

Show You The Way To Go

Words and Music by
Kenny Gamble and Leon Huff

227

Save Your Kisses For Me

Words and Music by
Tony Hiller, Lee Sheriden and Martin Lee

smile. I love you (I love you) all the while With your cute lit-tle wave, Will you

you. I love you (I love you) it's true You're so cute, hon-ey gee won't you

C   Cm   G   Am7

CHORUS

prom-ise that you'll save your

save them up for me your

kiss-es for me, save all your kiss-es for me

Am7/D   G   Bm

Bye-bye, ba-by bye-bye Don't cry hon-ey, don't cry Gon-na

G7   C   Cm   G

walk out the door but I'll soon be back for more Kiss-es for me save all your kiss-es for me

Am7   D7   G   Bm

229

so long hon-ey, so long. Hang on ba-by, hang on don't you

dare me to stay___ 'cos you know I'll have to say that I've know you've got to save your kiss-es for me,___ save all your

kiss-es for me ___ Bye-bye, ba-by bye-bye Don't cry hon-ey, don't

cry won't you save them for me___ ev-en though you're on-ly three.

Pearl's A Singer

Words and Music by
Ralph Dino, John Sembello, Jerry Leiber and Mike Stoller

and the lone - ly.
cut a re - cord.
Her job is
They played it

en - ter - tain - ing folks, ___ sing - ing songs ___ and tell - ing jokes
for a week ___ or so ___ on the lo - cal ra - di - o, ___

To Coda ⊕1

___ in a night - club. ___ Pearl's a
___ it ne - ver made it.

She want - ed to be Bet - ty Gra - ble

but now she sits there at that beer - stained

G/B   Am   D   G11   G

ta - ble —   dream - ing   of the things___ she nev - er got to do, __

G11   F   E   Am   G

___   all those   dreams ___   that nev - er ___ came true.

F   D7   G11   G7   C   F/C

D.S. al Coda   ⊕ **CODA**

Pearl's   a   night - club. ___

C   tacet. . . . .*   C   F   C

233

Rivers Of Babylon

Words and Music by
Farian, Reyam, Dowe and McMaughton

when we re-mem-bered Zi - on.   By the riv-ers of   For there, they that

carried us a-way in cap-tiv-i-ty,___ re - quir-ing of us a song. Now

how shall we sing the Lord's song___ in a strange land?   For there, they that

Group:

ah _____ (ah) _____

Let the words of our mouths and the med-i-ta-tions of our hearts be ac-cept-a-ble in thy sight here to-night. Let the

By the riv-ers of Ba-by-lon, there we sat down Yeah we

One Of These Nights

Words and Music by
Don Henley and Glenn Frey

Moonlighting

Words and Music by
Leo Sayer and Frank Farrell

He sees her at the same time — ev-er-y night At the Mex-i-can — Dis-co-teque

— She gives — him French kiss — es, — He gives — her French — ci-garettes. —

They sit at — the same ta — ble ev-er - y time, — The lights — are low — But their

eyes — shine — Just dig-ging the mu — sic from those sweet soul bands. — She keeps him out - a fights, Holds

on to his hands. He whispers slow— ly, "To-night's the night." Months — of plan— ning so it's

F G C

got-ta be right. Un-der the ta— ble her bag is burst-ing at the seams. She made— sure— to bring

F G7 C

ev - 'rything. Moon - light-ing, They're leav-ing ev -'ry-thing,— Moon - lighting, They're los-ing

F C G7

all their friends. Moon - lighting, It's the on— ly way.— It's fright'ning But it means—

C G7

—they'll stay— To - geth - er.— They're gon-na make it to - geth - er.—

F/C F C

His blue Morris van— is parked in an al— ley Just by Mon—ta-gue

Street.— His friend,— Ed-die, he did the re - spray —— So he couldn't drive it at all last—week—

—— And it cost most of the mo-ney that he had saved up To pay— Ed— die's re -

- ceipt, But he figures it's worth it— cos— the dis-guise is a must.— When they go missing they're gonna look for the van

Nine fif - teen Mon-day morn— ing at the print-ing works,— The boss no-tices some- one's not clocked in — And the wa-ter depart—ment of the coun— cil offices have a message That Missus Park's daugh- ter is missing.— Meanwhile the Carlisle turn off the M Six Mo-torway,— Drinking cold black cof— fee, eat-ing hot cup cakes,— She stares at him— with his beard unshaved,— Won-ders at his pow— er of staying awake.— He whispers low,—"You did just

fine!" They shared the driv— ing all— through— the night, She laughs —— "My mother will have lost her mind!—

A   A7   D   G

—— We're on-ly ten miles to Gretna, They're three hun-dred be-hind."- Moon - light-ing, They're leav-ing

A   D   G   D

ev-'ry-thing,— Moon - lighting, They're los-ing all their friends. Moon - lighting, It's the on——

A7   D

—— ly way.— It's fright'ning But it means— they'll stay. To - geth - er.—

A7   G/D   D

Repeat and fade

They're gon-na make it to - geth - er. ——————————————————— Moon -

G   D   A7 G A   A7

247

Love To Love You Baby

Words and Music by
Giorgio Moroder, Pete Bellotte and Donna Summer

there's no place I'd rath - er you be than with me here oh —

— oh love to love — you ba - by — oh

love to love — you ba - by — oh love to love — you ba - by —

do it to me a - gain and a - gain you put me in such an aw - ful spin, in a

Eb7(9b)   Ab   Dm7   G7

Cm7

F7(9b)   Bbm7   Eb7(9b)   Ab

lay your head down real close to me, Sooth my mind and set me free, set me

free - ee oh! ___ oh

F7(9b)   Bbm7   Eb7(9b)

Dm7   G7   Cm7

3 times

D.S. al Coda   ⊕ **CODA**

(Sexy Whisper) oh   love to love_you ba - by___   oh

Cm7

(Repeat & fade ad lib.)

love to love_you ba - by,   oh   love to love_you ba - by

Only Women Bleed

Words and Music by
Alice Cooper and Dick Wagner

all. On-ly wo-men bleed, on-ly wo-men bleed. On-ly wo-men

bleed. bleed.

Black eyes all of the time don't spend a dime ain't it a crime and

253

You there down on your knees_____ beg-ging me please ____ come watch me

bleed._____

1. On-ly wo-men__ bleed, on ly wo-men bleed. On-ly wo-men
2. (Instr.)
3. 4. (Vocal)

bleed,_____ on - ly wo-men bleed._____

D.S. al Fine
(Verse 1 only)

I Can't Stop Loving You

Words and Music by Billy Nicholls

'Cause I can't stop lov-ing you, I

can't stop lov-ing you No I

can't stop lov-ing you though I try,
(3) why should I try

Why should I try. I just

D.S. through to fade

Just For You

Words and Music by Alan Price

Knowing Me, Knowing You

Words and Music by
Benny Andersson, Stig Anderson and Bjorn Ulvaeus

Know-ing me, know-ing

D.S.
al

Repeat
and fade

Jolene

Words and Music by Dolly Parton

Fairly bright tempo

Jo- lene, Jo- lene, Jo- lene, Jo-

lene ———— I'm beg-ging of you, please don't take my man ————

Jo- lene, Jo- lene, Jo- lene, Jo-

-lene _____ please don't take him just be-cause you can _____

Cm   B♭   Cm

Your beau-ty is be - yond com-pare, with

Cm   E♭

flam-ing locks of au-burn hair, with iv-'ry skin and eyes of em-'rald green _____

B♭   Cm   B♭   Cm

Your smile is like a breath of spring, your

Cm   E♭

voice is soft like summer rain, and I can-not com-pete with you Jo-lene.

He talks a-bout you in his sleep and there's nothing I can

do to keep from cry-ing when he calls your name Jo-lene

And I can eas-'ly un-der-stand how you could eas-'ly take my man, but you

don't know what he means to me, Jo - lene. _____ Jo-

B♭ Cm

- lene, Jo - lene, Jo - lene, Jo - lene _____ I'm

Cm E♭ B♭ Cm

beg - ging of you, please don't take my man. _____

B♭ Cm

Jo - lene, Jo - lene, Jo - lene, Jo - lene _____

Cm E♭ B♭ Cm

please don't take him just be-cause you can.
ev - en though you

Bb   Cm

can.   Jo - lene

Repeat & fade ad lib.

Jo - lene

3. You could have your choice of men, but I could never love again.
He's the only one for me, Jolene.
I had to have this talk with you,
My happiness depends on you
And whatever you decide to do, Jolene.
(To Chorus)

Fool (If You Think It's Over)

Words and Music by Chris Rea

CHORUS

New born eyes_ al-ways cry with pain_ at the first look at the morn-ing sun_

Fool if you think it's ov - er, it's just be-gun._

Miss teen-age dream,_ such a _ tra-gic scene._

_ he knocked your crown_ and ran a - way._

First wound of pride ___ but how you cried ___

___ and cried ___ but save your tears ___ you've years and years. ___

Fool, if you think it's ov - er 'cos you said good-bye ___

___ Fool, if you think it's ov - er, I'll tell you why. ___

I'll buy your first__ good wine,_____ ooh, we'll have__ a real__

__good time_____ and save your cry - ing for the day.__

New born eyes__ al-ways cry with pain__ at the first look__ at the morn-ing sun__

Fade poco a poco

_____ Fool, if you think it's ov - er, it's just be-gun.__

Forever In Blue Jeans

Words and Music by
Neil Diamond and Richard Bennett

it don't walk.___ And long as I___ can have you here with me,___ I'd

much rath-er be___ for-ev-er in blue jeans.

Hon-ey's sweet.___ But it ain't noth-ing next to ba-by's treat.___

And if you par-don me,___ I'd like to say___ we'll do o-kay,___ for-ev-er in

blue jeans. May-be to-night.

May-be to-night, __ you and I __ all a-lone __ by the fire; __

noth-ing a-round __ but the sound __ of my heart __

__ and your sighs. __

Mon - ey talks. _ But it can't sing and dance _ and it can't walk. _ And long as I can have you here with me, _ I'd much rath - er be _ for - ev - er in blue jeans, babe. _ Hon-ey's sweet. _ But it ain't noth-ing next to

278

279

You Never Done It Like That

Words by Howard Greenfield
Music by Neil Sedaka

Moderately, in 2

Ooh ooh ooh ooh__ ooh ooh ooh ooh ooh__ ooh.

You're so ter - rif - ic;__ ooh,__ you nev - er done it like that.
My lips are burn - in';__ yeah,__ you nev - er done it like that.

You've nev - er been this way be - fore._____
I thought the flame was dead and gone._____

Show me the man _____ and let me shake his hand _____

Hey, look at me; _____ I feel just like Co-lum-bus. I did dis-cov-er you're _____ some kind of lov-er. _____

282

Lyin' Eyes

Words and Music by
Don Henley and Glenn Frey

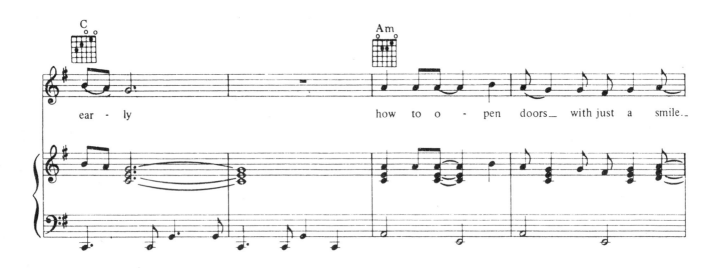

And it breaks her heart__ to think her love__ is on-
An - oth - er night,__ it's gon - na be__ a long__

ly
__ one;

giv - en to a man__ with hands__ as cold as ice.__
she draws the shade__ and hangs__ her head to cry.__

So she tells him she must go **out** for the eve -
My, oh my, you sure know how to ar -

You can't hide _____ your ly - in' eyes,

and your smile _____ is a thin ___ dis-

guise. I thought by now _____ you'd re - al - ize _____

_____ there ain't no way___ to hide___ your ly - in' eyes.___

Don't Give Up On Us

Words and Music by Tony Macauley

near - ly lost my head last night ___ you've got a right to stop bel - iev -

F   C/F   Bmsus4   Bm

-ing   There's still   a lit - tle___ love left   ev - en

A   C#/G#   F#m

D. S. al Coda

so   Don't give

D/E   F   D/E

CODA

through ____

rall.

A

I Will Survive

Words and Music by
Dino Fekaris and Freddie Perren

Fernando

Words and Music by
Benny Andersson, Stig Anderson and Bjorn Ulvaeus

Evil Woman

Words and Music by Jeff Lynne

make some miles_____ be - tween here and there. There's a

hole in my head_____ where the rain_____ comes in, You took my bod - y and played_____

_____ to win, Ha, ha wom - an it's a cry - in' shame, But you

ain't got no - bod - y else_____ to blame.

you found a fool ly - in' in a daze.___

Ha ha wom-an what you gon - na do,   You des-troyed all the vir - tues that the

Lord gave you,   It's so good___ that you're feel - in' pain   But you

D.S. al Coda

bet - ter get your face on board the ver - y next train._____

f

304

Evergreen

Words by Paul Williams
Music by Barbra Streisand

307

Daytime Friends

Words and Music by Ben Peters

-ed, and she needs____ a friend, so her

trem-bling fin - gers dial____ a tel - e - phone.____ (2) Lord, it hurts____

____ her o - ver there's no do-in' this____ a - gain____ he's the

best friend that her hus - band ev - er knew. When she's
long - ing for the way____ things should have been. And she

lone -   ly____   he's more than just a friend,____   he's the
won - ders   why some men nev - er find,____   that a

G   C/G   G   C/G

CHORUS

one she longs__ to give__ her bod - y to.____
wo - man needs__ a lov - er and__ a friend.__

Day-time friends

G   C/G   G   C/G

____ and night - time lov - ers,   hop - ing no - one else____ dis - cov -

G   C   G

— ers where they go,____   what they do, _____   in their se -

C   G   Em

Gone, Gone, Gone

Words and Music by
L. Russell Brown and L. Hayward

Moderately (with a double tempo feel)

It's a mys-te-ry   I can-not ex-plain,
I can't sleep at night,   got no ap-pe-tite,
on-ly things I got are heart-aches and pains.   She's gone, gone, gone gone.
ev-'ry-thing is wrong, but used to be right since she's gone, gone, gone gone.

Ooh yes, I tried to change her, —

tried to re-ar-range her per-son-al -i-ty. — Ooh

D.%. al Coda

but I'm pay-ing now I just can-not seem to face re -al -i-ty. —

⊕ *CODA*

(fade on repeat)

318

Da Ya Think I'm Sexy?

Words and Music by
Rod Stewart and Carmine Appice

Daddy Cool
Words and Music by Farian/Reyam

She's cra-zy like a fool

What a-bout Dad-dy cool? ___ I'm cra-zy like a fool ___

What a-bout Dad-dy cool ___

Dad-dy Dad-dy cool ___ Daddy Dad-dy cool ___

Daddy Dad-dy cool ___ Daddy Daddy cool ___

To Coda ⊕ 1.

2.

Dance, Dance, Dance
(Yowsah, Yowsah, Yowsah)

Words and Music by
Kenny Lehman, Bernard Edwards and Nile Rodgers

Head-in' t'wards the floor gon - na get down.
danc - in' with my ba - by drives me cra - zy,
A - get down some more.___
makes me ha - zy.___

Spoken
Rhum-ba___ and tang-o ___

Sing
Lat - in hus - tle too

Spoken
Yow sah yow sah yow___

Sing
___ sah   I wan - na boo - gie with you.___

to CODA ⊕
last time

Ba ba ba ba bow

D. S. 𝄋
al Coda

Fm7   Bb6   Fm7   Bb6

Fm7   Bb6

Bb6   Fm7   Bb6

Fm7   Bb6   Bb6

328

Nobody Does It Better

Words by Carole Bayer Sager
Music by Marvin Hamlisch

Blame It On The Boogie

Words and Music by
Elmar Krohn, Mick Jackson and Dave Jackson

Verse 3.
That magic music moves me, that dirty rhythm fools me
The devil's got into me through this dance.
I'm full of funky fever, a fire burns inside me,
Boogie's got me in its' super- trance.
(don't blame it on the sunshine etc.)

Chuck E's In Love
Words and Music by Rickie Lee Jones

You're So Vain

Words and Music by Carly Simon

344

Tryin' To Get The Feeling Again

Words and Music by David Pomeranz

try'n' to get the feel-ing a - gain. It seemed to dis-ap - pear as fast as it came.

I've been up, down, try'n' to get the feel-ing, I've been

up, down, try'n' to get the feel-ing a - gain.

Piano Man

Words and Music by Billy Joel

1. It's nine o - clock on a Sat - ur - day, The
(2. Now) John at the bar is a friend of mine, He
(3. Now) Paul is a real - es - tate nov - el - ist, Who
(4. It's a) pret - ty good crowd for a Sat - ur - day, And the

Sing us a song to - night.____

Well, we're all in the mood for a mel - o - dy.

And you've got us feel - in' al - right.____

D. C. al Fine

2. Now
3. Now
4. It's a

Rocket Man

Words and Music by
Elton John and Bernie Taupin

it's lone - ly out ___ in space. _____

on such a time

less ___ flight. _____

And I think it's gon-na be a long, ___ long   time ___ till touch-down brings ___ me 'round a-gain to   find ___

It's just my job five days a week. A rock-et

man, A rock-et man.

D.S. 𝄋 *al Coda* 𝄌

gradual cresc.

Coda 𝄌

Repeat and fade

And I think it's gon-na be a long, long time.

Repeat and fade

The Killing Of Georgie (Part 1 & 2)

Words and Music by Rod Stewart

2. His mother's tears fell in vain
The afternoon George tried to explain
That he needed love like all the rest.
Pa said, "There must be a mistake.
How can my son not be straight
After all I've said and done for him?"

3. Leavin' home on a Greyhound bus,
Cast out by the ones he loves,
A victim of these gay days it seems.
Georgie went to New York town
Where he quickly settled down
And soon became the toast of the Great White Way.

4. Accepted by Manhattan's elite
In all the places that were chic,
No party was complete without George.
Along the boulevards he'd cruise
And all the old queens blew a fuse;
Everybody loved Georgie boy.

5. The last time I saw George alive
Was in the summer of '75.
He said he was in love; I said, "I'm pleased."
George attended the opening night
Of another Broadway hype,
But split before the final curtain fell.

6. Deciding to take a shortcut home,
Arm in arm, they meant no wrong;
A gentle breeze blew down Fifth Avenue.
Out of a darkened side street came
A New Jersey gang with just one aim:
To roll some innocent passerby.

7. There ensued a fearful fight;
Screams rung out in the night.
Georgie's head hit a sidewalk cornerstone.
A leather kid, a switchblade knife,
He did not intend to take his life;
He just pushed his luck a little too far that night.

8. The sight of blood dispersed the gang;
A crowd gathered, the police came,
An ambulance screamed to a halt on Fifty-third and Third.
Georgie's life ended there,
But I ask, who really cares?
George once said to me, and I quote:

9. He said: "Never wait or hesitate.
Get in, kid, before it's too late;
You may never get another chance,
Cause youth's a mask, but it don't last.
Live it long and live it fast."
Georgie was a friend of mine.

We Are Family

Words and Music by
Nile Rodgers and Bernard Edwards

We are fam - i - ly. Get up, ev - 'ry - bod - y, and sing.

Liv - ing life is fun, and we've just be - gun to get our share___ of this world's

de - lights.___ High hopes we have___ for the fu - ture. And our

goal's in sight. No, we don't get de - pressed.___ Here's what we call___

364

I Was Made For Dancing
Words and Music by Michael Lloyd

Weekend In New England

Words and Music by Randy Edelman

Silver Lady

Words and Music by
Tony Macauley and Geoff Stephens

-ry-thing I put you through ___ but
___ love I had with you ___ and hon-ey, you're my last ___ hope and who else ___

Dm7   G   C

___ can I turn to? ___ Come on sil - ver la - dy take ___ my word. ___

F   G7   G11   C

I won't run out on you a-gain, ___ be-lieve ___ me. Oh I've seen the light ___ It's just one more

Em   F

___ night with-out you. ___ Here I am a mill-ion miles ___ from home.

G   G11   C

377

Instant Replay

Words and Music by Dan Hartman

mm woah - ho.— In - stant re - play,

{ got to have your love a-gain—
{ got me float - in' on a cloud—

1.

2.

Got me danc-in all a - round— all a- round all a- round— woo—

("Scat" vocal)

383

I Write The Songs
Words and Music by Bruce Johnston

mu - sic makes you dance___ and gives you spir - it to take a chance,___

And I wrote some rock 'n' roll___ so you___ can move.___

Mu - sic fills your heart,___ well, that's a real fine place to start.___ It's from me

it's for you, it's from you, it's for me, it's a world - wide___ sym - pho - ny.

At Seventeen

Words and Music by Janis Ian

I learned the truth at sev - en - teen___ that love was meant for beau -
(A) brown - eyed girl in hand - me downs___ whose name I nev - er could
(To) those of us who know___ the pain___ of val - en - tines that nev -

- ty queens___ And high school girls___ with clear - skinned smiles___ who
- pro - nounce,___ said, "Pit - y, please,___ the ones___ who serve,___ they
- er came,___ and those whose names___ were nev - er called___ when

sev - en - teen, I learned the truth.___ And
ha - ven for the eld - er - ly.___ Re -
ug - ly duck - ling girls___ like me.___ We all

those of us___ with rav - aged fac - es, lack - ing in the so -
mem - ber those___ who win___ the game___ lose the love___ they sought.
___ play the game___ and when___ we dare___ to cheat our - selves___ at sol -

- cial grac - es, Des - p'rate - ly___ re - mained___ at home___ in
to gain___ In de - ben - tures of qual - i - ty___ and
- i - taire___ In - vent - ing lov - ers on___ the phone,___ re -

Hit Me With Your Rhythm Stick

Words and Music by
Ian Dury and Chas Jankel

(2) In the wilds ___
(3) In the dock ___

hit me, hit me, hit me. Hit me, hit me,

hit me, hit me, hit me, hit me, hit me,

hit me, hit me, hit me.

394

Going In With My Eyes Open

Words and Music by Tony Macauley

blind - ly in _____ I fell and hurt my head _____
call me by _____ some - bod - y els - e's name _____

G

Oh I can't for - get _____ it but I won't re - gret _____
Oh I could - n't take _____ it I know it would break _____

F#m7   Bm   D/A

_____ it I could - n't ev - en stop it _____ if I
_____ it And I want to give you ev - ery - thing I

G   D/A   G/A

tried
am
On - ly this time I'm go - ing in with

A11   A   D   F#m7